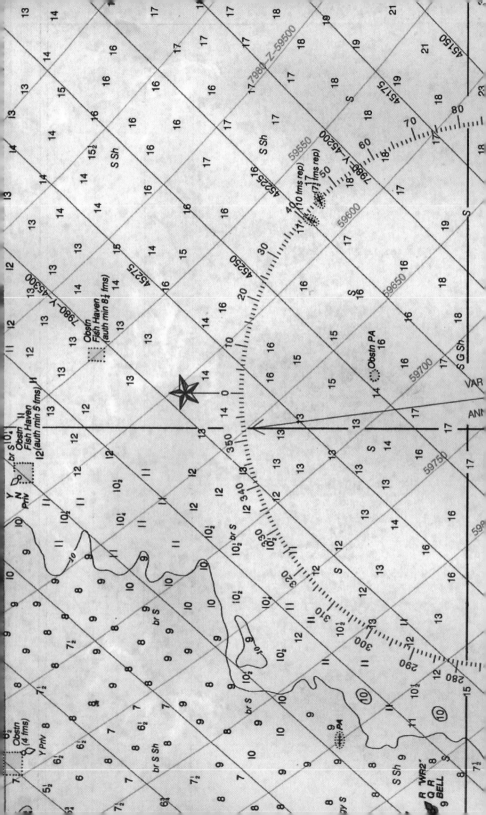

THE HUNDRED
FATHOM CURVE

THE HUNDRED
FATHOM CURVE

JOHN BARR

STORY LINE PRESS
1997

OTHER WORKS BY JOHN BARR

The War Zone
1989

Natural Wonders
1991

The Dial Painters
1996

for Bennington

Published by Story Line Press, Inc.
Three Oaks Farm, Brownsville, OR 97327

This publication was made possible thanks in part to the generous support of the Nicholas Roerich Museum, the Andrew W. Mellon Foundation, and our individual contributors.

Book design by M. Rae Thompson

Library of Congress Cataloging-in-Publication Data

Barr, John, 1943–
    The hundred fathom curve / John Barr.
        p. cm.
    ISBN 1-885266-38-3 (p).—ISBN 1-885266-43-X (c)
PS3552.A731837H86   1997
811'.54—dc21

A note on the title: The hundred fathom curve is the line of soundings used on nautical charts to mark the limits of the continental shelf and the beginning of the abyssal descent.

Thanks to the publications where these poems previously appeared.

PERIODICALS

Amelia, Terrapin; The Water Bed
Boulevard, Gloria Visits the Fry House
Confrontation, Deer Xing; Sign Shop, Sing Sing
Graham House Review, Flounder
Gray's Sporting Journal, Flyways
Harvard Magazine, St. Augustine, as In Florida
Indiana Review, The Brotherhood of Morticians
International Poetry Review, Exploring the Pastime Reaches
  and Beyond; poems from Articles of War, as The War Zone
Ives Street Press, Veterans Day, 1985 from Articles of War
Michigan Quarterly Review, The Dial Painters
New England Review and Bread Loaf Quarterly, poems
  from Articles of War
The New York Times, Restoration
Passages North, Restoration
Poetry Northwest, Jellyfish
Quadrille, Sign Shop, Sing Sing
Salmagundi, Wisteria
Western Humanities Review, Body Language, as Corpus

ANTHOLOGIES

*Anthology of Magazine Verse & Yearbook of American
  Poetry,* Restoration
Passages North Anthology,   A Decade of Good Writing
  Restoration

Special thanks to Bill Matthews, Molly Peacock and Stephen Sandy, poets from whom I learned, and to Carol Blinn.

CONTENTS

THE DIAL PAINTERS

ARTICLES OF WAR

NATURAL WONDERS

THE DIAL PAINTERS

The Brotherhood of Morticians

The story is told of the undertaker
who runs out of formaldehyde
and uses antifreeze instead.
Asked why his customers look blue,
he says he's made them good
for starting down to ten below.
Let me take that as my text tonight.

We function at the shelving edge between
the dead and living: upstairs receive
the bereft with sympathetic mien,
assist in the ceremonies that release
their grief, maintain decorum
from visitation to the Rest In Peace.
In small ways on this side
of the great divide we add valorem.

Down in the basement we prepare
the departed to deworld: fallen parts
put back, drain cavities, ensure
with needle and formaldehyde
that burial's not premature.
(Only we need know what's underneath
the suit; we're paid to work alone.)

Death we cannot forestall
for we come after, but the appearance of death,
we do. Not Jekyll, not Hyde, we undertake
to give the grievers back their own.
Not black, our arts are to restore:
toiletries and touch-ups, nails and hair.
Our charges seem to sleep. The wake,
correctly done, is a farewell
"to one who goes before."
Muted organ, muted lights, mute friends:
our insincere sincerity
buffers the bewildered family
from grim specifics of the tragedy.

Pinched in earthquakes, browned in fires,
consumed by cancer's radish,
a coronary's urgent turbulence,
collapsed at tables, choked on bones
(was there ever such savage disregard
as when Death squats, Neanderthal,
on the chest of a dinner guest?),
buckled in showers, felled at urinals.

Good fellows, our associates, Rotarians
who take the jokes as part of the job, who oversee
the motorcade, one stop upstream from Charon's,
the progress to the pit,
the vicarinvokingchrist's last words,
the family not hearing it,
the unaffected cemetery birds.
Or, if cremation's specified, they certify the burn,
entrust to a family friend the urn
to carry south to green reaching waters of the Gulf.

But the lesser in our trade
miss the magnitude of what we do.
We are after all not dressing meat.
Our task: no less than to preside
at a meeting of world and world, a mystery
wherein the person they knew
and some strange double coincide
("It's him, but it's not.").
In one, two worlds epiphany.

They're one of us still, the newly dead,
but lack their spark (that gone
to the parson's charge or who knows where).
The simmer in the brainpan at the body's end
is out. Stiffness invades the supple limbs.
The fresh dead season and dry.
And this is the first life after death.

Roots visit, tendrils touch,
slow solvents work new properties.
Animal, vegetable, mineral,
the dead in grave's grip reach
a dreamless crystalline estate.
A man, become his minerals, salts
away the last of his identity,
seeps to the water table and secretes
trace elements. And that is the next life after death:
a foreign stain on the littoral
at the beck of continental drift.

I tell you, World Without End is a statement of geology.
No longer lightning-life dotting the earth, marking divides,
we are returned to the planet's peristaltic beckonings,
welcomed by eons below, included in the crush and flow
of plate on plate, the tectonic thrust,
unimaginably strong and slow,
as continent mounts continent,
the grind, compression, conversion to what is next and new.

Divining the DuPage

From the high clay of the home hill
to Herlein's hearty bottomland,
along the DuPage River to the VFW,
then the long reach to Congregational ground
and back to the leached crown of your hill;
a slow progress over basement rock,
parsing impersonal beds of sediment,
standing waves of laval ooze, navigating
by sunken cars, by driven posts
I worry the good earth endlessly.

Wrinkling in distaste at toxic spills,
the asphalt apron of roads, I extract
goodness from grit (my enzymes equal
to hardpan's hardtack), relish the rare earth's
tincture of arsenic, tang of antimony.
Into invitational loam I graze:
sweet cilia of roots, made food
of compost, compilations of decay.

It being given that I live supreme
in a dark of my own making, lambent
under barn's manure, unseen by you
(unless by goose-stepping starling decapitated,
or straightened on your fishhook's J)
the better to work the still earth of your mind,
I sculpt in the earth's long cowl
a labyrinth of 20,000 leagues,
a hole continuous as history.

Extending with the motion of desire,
contracting as if shuddering,
see how I make love's elemental move.

Body Language

Arms implying one another,
legs in alternation going south,
this swaying scaffold of bones
bears through fields
the head without a thought.

❖

Blood floods the passageways,
the stomach grips its food,
the heart advances in darkness...

all while I walk,
shake hands, work the wash of events.

❖

In seven years, they say, it is renewed:
each hair in its follicle,
each pore in its microbe dell.
Atom for atom, the valleys of my brain,
the long journeys in my legs
suffer replacement.
A good occasion for improvement
you would think:

        but no,
          the same old scars,
            all my mistakes preserved.

❖

Once in his life
a man should know his body in its prime.

Dark drifts of hair,
the narrows of the waist,
the great junction of the thighs,
the torso lagged with muscle bronze.

The body's peak
on the long parabola from helplessness to helplessness.

❖

At death
the soul flies out of the mouth,
all eyes on it, it
continues out of the room.
Then the body is declared
larval to the man.

Yet I live in a settlement of two hundred bones.
Of its own accord my body beats.
Unmemorized
the great whorls of my fingerprints
approach like storms.

Gloria Visits the Fry House

Never firm the old Victorian,
perched on locust poles, poised
on beach's brink, begins to lean.
(Oddly the rusted chandeliers
are what appear to lean as they decline
to join the general lean to sea.)
With a great complaining of nails
rooms parallelogram, right angles
by the hundreds choose acute, obtuse.

The living room goes first: two picture windows
burst as the picture they were placed to contemplate
comes in the room. The main floor caves.
The upright red piano rolls
out the window, out to sea,
slowly righting to metacenter.
In the slow motion of demolition
walls fold down upon themselves
expressing volume room by room.
Dressers come up hard on seaward walls,
the bedrooms yield beds,
the third floor launches a pool table.
Like stalks the house's piping snaps:
water lines plume, gas lines effuse.

Eased by a wave, then waves,
the pile gets underway.
But rubble it is not.
Shedding cedar shakes like scales,
in the exploding surf it is reborn.
The Fry house joins the company
of things that put to sea.

St. Augustine

I saw the Portuguese men-of-war
shipwrecked like a treasure fleet
a solid mile along the shore.

Hard aground they tried to beat
to windward, set their living sails
this way and that around our feet.

A wave would sometimes climb the trails
of slime and lift one almost free,
then lapse and leave the pooled entrails.

We tried to flip one back to sea,
using a piece of board to help
dig under—unsuccessfully—

then left them, fouled for good in kelp,
the great blue spinnakers to gleam
and gesture, either after help,

or merely sailing their species' dream,
judging the distance as before,
keeping the middle of the stream.

Flounder

"During a period of rapid body changes
one eye migrates to the other side of the head,
after which the fish settles to the bottom."
                              —*Encyclopedia Britannica*

What hidden tackle moves one eye
to seek its opposite? What haul of muscle
gets it underway to navigate
shoals of the skull, to round the horn
in spite of how things are, how bone is,
in spite of the face the effort makes—
gargoyled, jury-rigged, mouth down-
hauled, eyes joined upwards as in prayer?

What sea change turns the world on its ear?
No longer the upright fish, proceeding
as if food and danger enter from the side,
what imbalance tips the scales, righting
only when right is up, left down,
the ability to see two sides
to things careened by a need to know
things at a distance, the distance of things?

No longer floundering, grown great
on beans of bottom sustenance,
you make the fisherman's day. At ease
to contours of the floor conformed,
you with a single vision see,
beyond the backlit dory, distant venues,
beyond the fishhouse catch of the day,
provender surpassing sole.

News

Listening to my portable at dawn,
I don't know what news is.
If I were the never-seen night editor
arriving in the wee hours to a ream
of copy—AP, UPI—
I wouldn't know where to begin.
Effluvia of muggings, what
the disgruntled boyfriend did,
a reply from State
rich with unreadable nuance:
How to separate the wheat from
what might all be wheat, how to choose
from yards of raw fact hardening
to history, how to decide
what is and isn't of significance.
Who How? What When Where Why!

This story on the *Amoco Achtung*
loses its bearings—deadline, by-line—
in the sound of surf improperly near.
I experience the slam, the fragility
of steel on rock's unreckoned fact.
Hard aground, I watch the dawn, the gulls,
the crude unloading on the swells.
Failing to probe the failure to act,
to inquire as to an Inquiry,
my piece would end: "Last on the highline,
the Captain (not even his name!) had nothing to say
about the ultimate bad day at sea."

Or this Wisconsin bulletin.
Worth a mention at most, the "Record Kill"
reminds me of my one hunt: 3 A.M.,
unpacking guns whose names echo
like shots (REM-ing-ton, WIN-ches-ter),
the architecture of the breech, the flow
of walnut into steel, the oiled action
taking each brass bullet in.

You never see deer coming: they appear.
Incapable of awkwardness, their caution
passing for intelligence, if these
were people I'd be drawn to them.
Bam. A drunken dance and fall.
Then, mammal on mammal, I give with my knife
until the cornucopia lets go.
The neck has lost its arch of character,
the question mark it carried in life.
The carcass assumes the shapes my work dictates.
Hung by the neck, it strains to know
the branch from which it heavily depends.
My hands, blood bright, have dried to ocher,
the color of the paintings in caves
which this account approximates.

Still he, the editor,
I put my copy in and disappear.
At six, clock radios connect
New York's need for
time and need for news:
the people wake.

And thereby are my poems my news.

The Dial Painters

"Over the past two decades, the bodies of at least
a dozen women who once painted watch and clock
dials with radium have been laid out here
for a final measure of radioactivity."
— *The Wall Street Journal*
September 19, 1983

Pointillistes,
you made your points punctiliously
(big hand, little hand, 1, 2, 3...)
made faces readable on wrists,
in bedside dark.

Chorus of good girls, busy bees,
waiting for the whistle's blow
you painted your toes day-glo,
seeing the possibilities
clowned circles on your cheeks, in jest

egressed
like wraiths, the best
of spirits. From afar
townspeople could remark
the green fire in your hair.

Twirling in lips
the radium tips,
unaware your brushes were
with death,
how could you, hazarding a hair-

line numeral,
know that you enlightened yourselves as well?
Seldom has artist been
so taken by his work,
seldom illumination seen

so unintentional
or unconventional.
Elgin ladies, your bones protest
that marking time at best
is hazardous to health.

By the time
it dawned on you that to ingest
even a trace of these trace elements
involved grave consequence,
you were possessed:

Host to an unholy ghost
who farmed your flesh for tumor's bloom,
who made of your skin a palimpsest,
who made of your bones a metronome
that beat time to the stars.

Slightly to our chagrin
you showed mere industry—
punching out, punching in—
can gain the immortality
the rest of us quicken for.

Mute furies,
interred in the circle of the clock,
you roam
as Greek as tragedies
the stations of your zodiac.

Saints of our time,
Mme. Curie's
curiosities,
to the leaden ark containing your phosphor
skulls, italicized bones we come.

Alive with salts
whose half-life
is your afterlife,
in university vaults
you shine for thousands of years.

Sign Shop, Sing Sing

Worthy of Dante, penal planners
fit the sentence to the crime.
One hundred times the lifer writes DEAD END
the rapist YIELD
the parolee GOODBYE AND COME AGAIN.

Consigned to help us KEEP RIGHT
these minor Moses lay down laws
     ONE WAY
     OBEY THE LIMITS
     MERGE

In bins wait cautions
     FROST HEAVE
     FALLING ROCKS
for every hazard but the one that put them here.

We hear and heed. Mild souls who hold the road,
the likes of us imagine the likes of them,
in a custom '57 Chevy,
mowing down every sign they've made
on the way to unpaved, unposted roads.
And wouldn't we like, like them, to open up,
looking for conviction in the zone
between boredom and extinction.

Driving in Rain

End of a weekend, going back,
my two tracks sinuate as one.
Skin of rain drawn tight by wind,
the windshield wipers don't keep up.

Posed in this airspace, passing
Purgatory Gulf Pop. 125,
I wonder why observe the limits, why
keep pulling it back,
when, let go, it would go
straight for a time,
                          then wander
off without assumptions,
questioning first the need for road.

Diving the East River

NYPD divers, who like their work,
can't like diving the murk of what New York
has urinated, belched, expressed.
I think of them, rather, as men who lower
to the actual to see how it compares.

Chalk to *mouse* to *charcoal* they see
feelingly the dropped this, thrown that.
Ooze rich in shopping carts, cash registers,
cars—"quite a few occupied"—
always they find that what they can imagine
falls short of what drops off Manhattan's table.

Crime is the excuse for these descents
which we lack license to attempt,
but where else can the living
walk the bottoms of their dreams?

At earth's edge, where streets cease,
the river that is East plows south,
under the urge to be Atlantic
carries the question to sea.

The Water Bed

Asleep on the deep, adrift
on a wedge of inland sea
one foot by six by three,
I see my singular craft
intend for open ocean.

Not in accord, the bed and I,
a study in the laws of motion:
wayward the bag of H_2
O, opposite, equal to
my every move. However sly

each kick provokes a kick in kind,
each turn in turn turns me. Supine to prone,
starboard to port, whatever the move,
a moment behind
comes a gurgle...an answering heave...a groan.

By turns the weather grows untoward.
"Eight bells.
Barometer falls.
What is not moored
in cabin moves. I fear a blow."

Your ship is in distress.
Having shipped its weight in seas,
it answers less and less.
Having sent your SOS,
you next would choose to be:

( )capsized, ( )aground, ( )overboard as chum
for what patrols below (assume a shark).
I cling in the dark
to the hope that *( )none of the above*
may be my kingdom come.

Becalmed. (Be calm. The surface
tension simulates a mirror's face:
So long as no muscle moves, dry land.)
Under the sky's braised bowl,
slack flap of sail

hum hymns. Quote homilies.
On the gunwhale, notched with days,
keep notes for your best-selling return.
Plan a perfect crime.
Compose this poem.

Hallucinate judiciously.
Tan and thin, be vain.
Think hygroscopic; accept the salt lick's lip.
Decline assistance from any ship
not going your way.

"Chichester here...weak but clear.
Three hundredth day...down to last...
rigged sail from pages of diary...no mast.
Pet fish, Turbot, taken by skate.
My words for history: Oh great...."

Wait for the trades, the ironware wind,
for the water troubled by its hidden hand.
Wester on the riffling rush.
Abide the body's anguished English.
Accept, from night's high noon,

the vast black pointed with all the stars
in statement out of deep time.
Enormity as friend,
watch how they precess,
dead reckon by their trend.

I am boarded by a prize crew:
Ahab wrapped in Elmo's fire,
the Ancient Mariner,
still albatrossed, still not a listener,
Bluebeard as always talking revenue.

Together we listen to
the bong of the Lloyd's bell for the overdue,
swap yarns of the literary wrecks we've known:
The Hesperus, Deutschland, Gloria Scott
("Great Scot! Dred Scott, scot-free, dreads Gloria's cot.").

Ocean, vessel, cargo:
Le Bateau Ivre, now the three,
moves to make a fourth of me.
Sunk in the hold of the vinyl valve,
I watch my body do a slow dissolve,

the fields of skin clear,
deposits of tallow, calcium,
the underlying tenderloin
of *Gray's Anatomy* appear,
limbs unlimn, the entire bridgework of bone

(*"the hip bone connected to the...thigh bone"*)
wrist catch, arm boom, neck davit, knee
unship from symmetry—
"Goodbye, articulated spine.
Exclamatory ribs, *allons*!!"—

the hands release,
the stomach, its own small water bed, from
oblate butterball deform,
the anal bud untense,
the groin lose its significance.

My brains unbell.
Brown hair platinum,
the face below the face three-quarters full,
my clarifying eyes descry
the organs at their alchemy.

My three parts water find
their fourth. I unrind.
Decked out in water dress,
swell wearing a vinyl rag
or body bag,

I am in the way of water versed.
I share its fascination with extreme:
Chased to mist, destabilized to steam,
sent forward to water futures, rain
or (a study in motion's steady state) pack ice.

Poetical tars, unable to refrain
from a life on the bounding main,
find your level or find your sleep.
Learn from the fate of *The Crippled Quatrain*.
Commit your legends to the deep.

Restoration

I love to recover the quality
of things in decline.
To scour stone, scale paint from brick,
to compel, with wire brush,
the flourish wrought by iron.
To refinish wood, solving for
forgotten grain.
To give, by weeding, our stone wall
back its dignity.
To left and right the borders of our lot,
to square the corners of our keep.

I have even dreamed: pushing a pushcart,
I stop anywhere and start
doing what needs to be done.
The first building takes time:
replacing windows, curing the roof.
I know compromises must be made
and make none, a floor at a time.

I work along an interstate
a century after Johnny Appleseed.
A modest people makes me chief.
(They, too, enjoy the hazy shine
of finished work by last light.)
Storm drains relieved, brick walks relaid,
a heritage of dust and wrappers
is renounced. The square square,
trim trim, the town for once
is like an artist's conception of the town.

ARTICLES OF WAR

I.

Our lean no-nonsense hull bears west
invading Tonkin Gulf
                    like a sliver in the blood.

In thirty days we see three hours of sun,
the rolling never stops not once.
New Year's Eve we celebrate
refueling into heavy seas.
Our Christmas presents dangle a week late
in the dark rush between.

"I know that men of goodwill everywhere join me
in extending to every man and woman of the Pacific Fleet
best wishes for a merry Christmas and a happy New Year."

Posted below: a picture from the *Times*
of the flag in flames in Central Park.

II.

The coastline edges to the edge of our chart.
We move on a central, generous blue.
Wind high, ocean plain smack
tonnage our bow plows through,

the boiling salt excitement of our wake,
gone in minutes,
then birds on our bobbing crates
a thousand miles from land.

To pass the time
I try to teach our bosun mate
"Sailing to Byzantium."
Good-natured, he laughs and laughs.

It is by no means enough that an officer o
f the Navy should be a capable mariner. H
e must be that, of course, but also a grea
t deal more. He should be the soul of tac
t, patience, justice, firmness and charity
. No meritorious act of a subordinate sho
uld escape without its reward, even if the
reward is only a word of approval. Conver
sely, he should not be blind to a single f
ault in any subordinate though, at the sam
e time, he should be quick and unfailing t
o distinguish error from malice, thoughtle
ssness from incompetency, and well meant s
hortcoming from heedless or stupid blunder.

I hand it to you, Guthry
(*hydraulic   liberty risk   at fault*),
you made it hot for the child officer,
by his narrow gold stripe circleted.

What I don't know hurting me,
I sharpen the edges of the being in the bunk.
In red light, rows of rivets gleam.
I'm on an unsafe dream.

III.

In this dream warships, mammoth as carriers but without
engines, drift on rivers and seas. Only when two chance to
drift together can the tribes do battle, swarming as the hulls
bump and carry apart again. If two of the great ships lodge
together in a cove or bend of river the tribes will fight to
extinction. But mostly they drift alone long periods of time...

From fumy sleep I go up ladders.
In the dark pilot house:
"I relieve you." "I stand relieved."

The ship's interior—hatches, scuttles,
passageways—holds in a welded maze
unmoved from when the ship was built.

The men, tiered in aluminum bunks,
are far away, each one
working a one-man mine for opals.

A star says star. The deck says steel.
The bow, equal to weathers, parts only air.
Above, behind, the radar seeks.

Milkshine fills the binocular field.
Sparkling with salt, the ship pushes
through seas of simultaneity.

IV.

I stare down into waterburn.
This urge to enter what we see.
Unrefracted tropical sun
with its whole arm
works deeply the ocean interior.

Water and light in union
make a third thing—color as fluid
deepened endlessly.
Into the quarry of aquamarine,
high-walled with light, the mind high dives.

My fingers cleave watersilk.
I breathe heavy light.
The big cavitation of the props
gone by, my struggling stops, my slowed

descent, in diminishing light,
gains the country where the shark
is eagle, fish the fishermen, and men
no more than stones along the road.

V.

In spite of electronics, this ritual endures.
Holding a sextant as old as an astrolabe,
the navigator looks for stars.
This is a twilight business.
Only in the minutes when both
horizon and star are visible,
can he shoot the altitude of Sirius.

Later stars, ragged bundles
that emerge only in night's full text,
meteors' quick scars,
how light in a thin rain falls
and our eyes, better than sextants,
fathom a drift of protons on the face,
are of no interest to the navigator.

VI.

Spectacle, dumb show, *idiot savant*
uncaged in a no-man's land, it
lunges, swings with slow recovery
until, to the pull of a distant absolute
responding, the knowledge in its atoms,
overshooting each time less—lightly
but persistently on this one point—
settles on what is true.

Then in three degrees of freedom
it remembers. Coins and watches,
our rolls and recoveries
do not dispel its equilibrium.
Housed in a binnacle, lit from below,
its amber radiance includes the helmsman's face.

VII.

Good men, who eat their cubic mile of cold,
their biscuits of loneliness without complaint,
bad boys, who never finished school
but welcome the war zone for the extra pay.

For the various ocean on which they work
they show no feeling, only the respect
lumberjacks would show a leaning tree.
Waterspouts, whales pass distantly.

The "youngsters," down in the hold with dreams,
don't hear the pumps reciprocate with steam.
The old men, repair their only art,
no longer follow arrivals and departures of the heart.

Each makes a pact with steel,
comforted in the mesh of part and part.
They never age: machinery maintained,
they seem by that to be sustained.

Before agreeing to a Sailor's Home,
they would put to sea once more
and, far out, lay the fires
and give the ship into the hands of drift.

VIII.

Mike boats grumble and start their runs
out to merchants, red with running rust,
destroyers named for heroes.
They lift and settle on the light,
on delicate chains swing seaward on the ebb.
In early morning
they weigh anchors and depart.

Fare thee well, my bonnie girl,
I can no longer stay.
I'm off on a trip on a government ship
ten thousand miles away.

IX.

As a treeman descending a fir, with chain saw
uncreating it by lengths,
composes the hole in space which he climbs down,
so I am the treeman and you
the needle-perfect absence of the fir.

Arty and not true. In my bunk,
in metaphysical conceit I reach
your latitude. I anchor off yr coves,
I land, I take yr breasts' unleavened loaves
in my two hands. I eat my solitude.

Satisfying, still not true.
You are blue letters doused with Shalimar.
You are the welcoming warmth I write into.
You are the suede, Wisconsin jacket I put on
in spite of regulations. As far from you

as it is possible on earth to be,
I see you in your sweater that's soft brown,
teaching piano in Madison.
You are, in this blossoming
of incompletion, where I fail to be.

X.

SALVATION, THIS IS TWO-SIX CHARLIE.
YOUR TARGET ZERO FIVE, FIVE SIX,
HUTS AND TROOP ENTRENCHMENTS.
FOUR GUNS, FOUR SALVOS,
HIGH EXPLOSIVE, OVER.
THIS IS SALVATION. READY, OVER.

Our sailors cradle the fifty-pound round
into the tray. The breechblock shuts.
The gun slams like an explosion in the next room.
Used to it, the sampans don't even move
when our muzzles unburden above their heads.

The mountains, too, absorb the round,
plunging the jungle's triple canopy.
Says Two-Six Charlie in his floating plane:
YOU BARBECUED A COW WITH THAT ONE.

XI.

We listen to a strike go in,
watch the copper twinkle of flares,
hear the pilots mark "On top."

Bombs drop out of no category
into no pattern. I don't know,
they shoot back,
the pilots note the flak offhand,
we take it in like kids at a picture show.

I don't know, a bend of river, sampans
maybe maybe not with contraband,
the great jet's angle of dive, the pilot's thumb
all come to a coincidence.

Then, too far to hear,
heat lightning there   and there, there.

XII.

The plane in pieces raining down
thy kingdom come
the flyers, nothing more to fly in, fall.

Then our ship turning in the fog,
searching the small black waves around.

Out of the weather in the hangar bay
I stoop to the debris.
The ruined gear gives back
a warmed, rank smell of sea.

Wing flap with flak holes
Orange, buoyant seat pads
Crushed helmet with fittings torn away

Lacking its head, the helmet
is him here, the man I didn't meet,
whom I may not have liked,
who may have said *Jesus* in surprise
when the world bucked and let him through.

XIII.

For us no harm, no lost limb
or crushed bone.
The Gulf a theater,
we audience to our own
bombardments.

The weather was mild.
That spring birds came to the ship.
At night we smelled the landwind
and imagined new animals
couched in the dark under bare branch.

A great curve downward and away,
the earth returns us to our loves.
A warm wind pesters the ship.
It's time to wake reliefs.

NATURAL WONDERS

The Orb Weaver

In the pre-dream of Creation—dingo
savanna, crab surf, serpent arroyo—
I was assigned thicket and air.
Whitetail taught to flee dissent,
coyote to collapse on his prey,
right whale to mouth his meadow's krill,
my trick, to make one thing repeatedly.

Out of this orifice unheard-of muscles
press a cable mile, 8 hands pay out
in junctions that I simply know.
I steeplejack an undulant array's,
a billowing acre's, rungs and radials.
From the host of brother structures in genetic gel,
my radical dance deduces one recalling
by moon the tenor of rails, by noon's blue hole
the 20/20 of a clean kill.

As language was given to man that he may have
dominion yet again, my web
like metaphor its hold makes good on air:

compass rose of indirection,
proof of an occult geometer,
dread nought, round hosanna,
shout of spacial glee.

After the maker's heart
I put the merest gloze on air.
Having sutured nothing—nothing
nearly nothing still—I frame
a reference for the flying folk.

Lighthousekeeperlike I tend
this hazard feet above the forest floor.
Each few days, the lattice rent
and apparent with dew, I eat it and renew
(word made flesh, made fresh) its invisibility.

My hands take hold of certain strands,
I settle to see what comes my way:

arielles and tinkerbelles,
a butterfly under double flags of truce,
manic mosquitos, a hoplite bee,
a Mack truck Luna hit the silk.

What happens next, whether to tiny tocsins
or large beats of alarum to come on the run,
whether to spring, fang, decant
is left, I believe, entirely to me.

I see a watchworks, socketed and sprung,
and I say "jewelled movement, motionless."
Immune to vertigo, I say "excused from gravity."
I see my causeways littered with body bags
and I say "Form is hunger, hunger form."

Jellyfish

Brought in to the feet of the piers,
this thing succeeds the hurricane.

Hung in a dome
four sacs, a ruffle intestine
all in gelatin,
distended, calm.

Lordlike the rim flagella beckon in
a freighter's melon, swollen bread-bits.
Stoved boats litter shore. This thing shows up
like a bishop who survived the overthrow.

Terrapin

Last night we used him for a centerpiece.
"Pet Rock" "Rubbleman" "Sepulcher Sam"
Our Brobdingnagian wit fazed him
not a bit. The wonder is that life informs
the carapace (big black and pumpkin chips),
the legs that tractor earth's unevenness,
the serpentine head, at all.
Only the eye—and it a slit of semiprecious
light—looks other than conglomerate.

Having no place for shelf life
we keep him casually corralled
(Does he go snow-blind in the sink?),
include him in what we do.
But the household god steadfastly will not eat
our offerings of parsley, meat;
for hours holds head extended or a claw
as if reverted to his quarried
origins, the living rock.

Perhaps he's trying to hibernate
in a winter our warmth will not provide.
Or refuses, always, to respond
for reasons of turtle dignity.
Or fears to be soup, or hopes to lithify
remembering how good it was in the Jurassic.
The life within withdrawn, he's comatose—
or raptly attends some call we cannot hear.

Clearly we're tuned to different frequencies:
the elder species and the parvenu.
Today you put him out for air
in the turtletight backyard, returned
to find him—allichazaam—not there.
And as he was elsewhere when among us,
now he is a presence in his absence.

Suburban Triptych

I.

No house outlasts its hill.
Here, especially, fifty years will see
bones, the basement scar,
something in its place.

But for now the half-moons of the hammer's miss
could have been carpentered yesterday;
kernels of resin sweated from joists,
still soft to the thumbnail, shine.
In the room where the well probes the hill's heart
the tank, full of taking, sweats.
The furnace waits, one thing on its mind.

II.

Excavating for a septic tank,
my father shovels a rock from eight feet down.
"That's never been touched by human hands."
I hold it aloft: for history,
the cold white thing from genesis.

Green algae, heavy hair
we pitchfork from the pond by wagon-loads.
In a week it dries to nothing, to stink.
Too many turtles, my father hooks one, clips
off its head with pruning shears, tosses
the astonished body on the compost heap.
Our garden yields a crop of trilobite
and sea-worm (already dreaming stone
when glaciers crushed their seabed into soil):
dead ringers for the fat tomato worms
we hunt. In the green immediate
they burst and soak into thirsty dirt.

III.

Past grass, past banjo legs of insects
into loam; six inches down, moraine;
then, lodged in the towering clay,
deep in the hill's dome, be still:

You hear small gravel. Burrowing.
Then nothing.
Then
a breathing other than your own,
so slow
the breathing in
continues from one glacier to the next.

Hunting for a Tool

I stand by the basement shelves
breathing the odor of the mouse who died
of love for cardboard, powders or tar.
Here is sandpaper with its bite of wood,
bottles with labels telling what to do.
No carpenter, I go to the bins below.

Early TV's, radios built like chapels,
vacuum tubes with silvered skulls.
My father accumulated in the dream
of hams: to tune the babble of frequencies—
Augustan time checks...the BBC
—to make Marconi's leap
and travel in the company of light.

I relish the clean-cut teeth of gears,
a rheostat devoid of ohms.
A magnet feeling steel still pulls.
A lump of lead still wraps the hand
around itself, expressing heft.
Still waiting for its proper use,
a light bulb rattles its tungsten tongue.

Bird Voice in the Halls of 5 A.M.

theebro eebro   *eebro*

In the mild dark
the radiator is with difficulty white.

eebaw   *eebaw*

The syllables vary like a signature.

kohl kohl   *kohl*

A new voice tries
the uvular, diphthong
of its particularity.
Fricative, apocope, an insectic click
join the tuning symphony.

Again the chance
to go forth on the soft lawn,
to take, like my sprinkler,
differing angles to the ground,

to the *Aw*   *Aw*
of a bitumen crow in hemlock
give *jambo,* the greeting in Swahili,

to *each   each   chip chik*   *epeleeklaw*
                                        chaw

reply in the lingua franca *tjonn   tjohn.*

In the Carboniferous House

In the Carboniferous House
a pillar of gnats stands in the absence
of a prophet's glance, dragonflies flirt
with forever amber. In the Herpeterium
Dimetrodon, under improvised sail,
duck-billed Hadrosaur, helmet-
headed Pachycephalosaur
show you don't need brains to inherit the earth.
Gigantopithicus (9' 600 lbs)
shows what the marsupials might have done.
(Jurassic shrews, amounting to nothing, wait their turn.)

In the Zoo of the Extinct, passenger
pigeon rises to no final gun,
the competition among grasses is suspended.
Unaware of the weathers in wait, fry
of Ichthyosaur people Wyoming seas,
amphibia skedaddle in imbricate surf.
Armorial skulls, shelled dead ends, the treasured
thumb, the oops, the overtaken, overcome
shelter this side of extinction's brink.

In Noah's Park, Latin remembrancers
name the 28 orders, Odysseus asks
last questions, panzers plan their vector.
At the Ice House a keeper sweeps,
his Edsel parked outside.

Things in the dark
exist but are not realized.
Perhaps with wings
they wait for enacting light.
I start out as the sky descends
to the visible spectrum and begins.

Midmorning I find in a lab
a blue magnetic fluid:
revolving in the stress of gauss,
the source of blue resides.
November nights, up to the first snow,
derive from this seat of blue.

I spend a month reflecting at Palomar.
My delicate fourteen tons
I bring to bear
on galaxies: their lonely shine
harbors
on my dustless, understanding curve.

I come to a mountain out of season.
The brass bench mark telling the height
is under ice.
Without witness, without cease
a blizzard
pummels the summit's face.

I reach the pole. Here at the axis
the wobble and grind is audible.
My compass tries to point straight down.
It, too, deceived: Having achieved
one absolute, the source of north,
to find that south surrounds, is all but it.

The Humboldt Current has my boat
and its mile of line straight down.
Now and then, fishermen haul in
the inexplicable
along with seabream, haddock, squid.
I hook a coelacanth, thought long
extinct, and brain it with an oar.

Nose to the bottom
I shove off from the hundred fathom curve.
Slow footage of mud unreeling through my mind,
the miles of decline become my age.
Hauled up someday by accident,
rupturing in the lost pressure,
my look will say how knowing feels.

Living among the trilobites
I learn you cross great lengths of time
by stilling the waiting in yourself.
From scavengers I see how you can live
off your own dead kind.
I gum the grit of a tidal flat
and have no name.

A chance letter brings me home,
telling how I was found.
Returned I sit
like water in a jar,
light from a window passing through,
a slow rain of precipitate
remembering the bottom.

Teamsters

Now must be the time to make time,
judging from the rapid bump of semis
filling my room. (Having discharged live loads
at Albany are they—at 4 A.M.—
on to loads of cold-rolled sheet?)

At All-Night Stops, in the presumptive day
of mercury vapor, you see them circling their rigs,
testing with ballpeen for the "No flat here"
that 18 Firestones better sing;
you overhear them in booths, in the assumed
accent of crackers prolonging
a mythology of getting through.

In shirt tails and shit kickers, awkward
as crabs, no wonder their withdrawal
into the greater identity of cabs.
Atop chrome registers they double clutch
in intricate shifts, feel in gear trains
for the nodes to make this mother move.

Muncie...South Bend...Kankakee,
on handfuls of speed they test the limits:
Smokey's temper, templates of curves,
tread's griplessness on ice,
the harebrained, hairpin possibilities.

Eating the rinse their mudflaps fling,
I can ignore how they highball our good grief,
what their bumpers say they pay in taxes,
even the menace of their Brotherhood.
Bring our bread with incivility
they may, but (under their seats the proper answer
for highjackers) bring us our bread they do.

Deer Xing

Sitting on sixty, we moved through Illinois.
In fast slow motion, farm by farm,
Wisconsin, like a realm whose deer
dream cars and leap, came near.

They panic, the wardens say,
but this one was intent,
crossing a lane to charge. The impact
of a deer in the air was a near wreck.
With a buckled front, but otherwise no harm,
we stopped and backed.

Sprawled in the ditch, wide-eyed,
the doe looked surprised that it had died
instead of us. As if that was the accident.

Wisteria

"Mm," I thought, of your slash-and-burn approach
to pruning. "Cut to the bone of bark, this one
won't come back." Here at summer's end
I am informed of my mistake.

Not sooners, not Jack's bean,
not the Persian Expedition
or the Crown of Thorns
infestation of Pacific reef
bests this vegetable version of eruption.

Out of the ground in a surround of trunks
merged half to tree, hand over hand
up downspouts, stucco, the failed copper of gutters,
green creepers the windows barely hold
at bay declare, from the antenna's mast,
a quarter of the house rattanned.

Even now new shoots depart the mother bundles,
like biplanes execute slow rolls, shallow
dives, the stall. Their leaps of faith—of six feet,
more—into the yonder of their kind
try for anything at all: the lob,
the double helix, the lazy eight of infinity.

In lieu of sight a sure touch for what
comes next, they find the grounds for another try
or fail, canes braiding themselves to rope
in vacancy. They base in air
small Permian fronds, refreshingly thornless;
lavender puffs the blunt bees bore and buss.

Under the overhang, overwhelmed, I write
"Offspring of wistful and hysteria.
God in my garden, rooted good."

Still Life

Standing out of time, the

> "porcelain bottle
> monochrome *sang de beouf*
> K'ang Hsi, early 18th c."

does better than the bronzes whose verdigris comes
        from a compromise with air,
than silver under nightfall of tarnish,
or iron, fresh-cut the color of daylight,
        but soon recouped to rust,
the cup the crack travels a millimeter
        the millenium,
tapestries larvally tatterdemalion,
the rest of this place losing its grip to
        arms of the damp, acids of air, pell
        of the particulate.
The ceramic hull does better than the Liberian
        charter whose economics preclude paint,
and the potter who, the story goes, unable to please
        the emperor with more of the blood-red ware
        that occurred when a pig wandered into his kiln,
        himself jumped in, in despair, thereby repeating
        the right reducing atmosphere.

From sleep in the hill, long weathering, the levigation
        of the basins;
thrown in a time of peace between pressures from the East
        and pressures from the West;
compelled by the unlabored decisions of hands to bloom;
it excels in the way it avoids excess:
debased court tastes, self-imitation, virtuosity.

From its base it plums for an ordinary use,
but gathering to the top of its round
it turns, at the same time, into neck,
continuing to rise and taper,
and refuses, at the top, to flare.

From the family of reds found by copper

>   *sacrificial red*   *tea dust*
>   *sky-clearing red*   *soufflé*
>   *ox-blood*   *liver*
>   *rust*   *coral*

comes this bing cherry from the accidents of fire.

Displayed in a case
made of Wisconsin molecules, assembled in Queens,
it bears to futures that will welcome it or not
red chemistry and a musical note.

Flyways

I used to think of them as marathoners
raised to a power of ten: seemingly
indefinitely able to postpone
over Olympic hauls (four, five thousand miles,
a quarter of the globe's waxed face)
the need to flop down, flabby with exhaustion
and wait for rest, in its own good time,
to bring a better state of being.

After the bouillon of Canadian lakes in bloom,
fingerlings grown too big, air filled with lateness,
they lift, taking in stride the variegated land,
brick bunkers of the Bronx, the lay of Central Park,
giving room to LaGuardian pterodactyls,
the prickle of hunters on the Chesapeake
with their coy deceits, out over open ocean,
the earth's hull visible...

the camber and bell and hollow bone
(as grasped in the sienna studies of Leonardo)
working well, minute adjustments of the tail
with inertial certainty

                              keeping well to the right
the wrinkle of burnt Sierras, one side snow;
the desert incised by rulered roads,
by rounds of irrigated green; large-mannered Mexico,
the Mayan rhythms gathering to isthmus—

until you pointed out, two days ago,
that neither does the heart (not the "heart"
but the heart as grasped in the dissections
of Michelangelo) need rest, seemingly
indefinitely able to maintain
a heading and speed, resting as it goes,
through day's distractions, night's curing cold,
inclement weathers of every sort

until, after years of regularity,
it comes to a Patagonia not seen before;
landing in this new non-flying it doesn't need,
it joins in the clamor of its kind;
on shingle, inhospitable but free of predators,
just above the surf's antarctic burn,
it assumes the nesting rights established
when the pole was elsewhere and the continents one.

About the Author

John Barr was born in Nebraska in 1943 and grew up in Illinois. Graduating from Harvard College in 1965, he served for five years as a Naval officer on destroyers and made three cruises to Vietnam. Returning to Harvard for an MBA, he graduated a Baker Scholar in 1972. Since then he has pursued parallel careers as poet and investment banker. As businessman John Barr has been a Managing Director at Morgan Stanley and has founded three companies, including the country's largest natural gas marketing company and a prominent investment banking boutique. As poet he has published widely in literary journals and in three books published in fine press editions by Warwick Press.

John Barr is President of the Poetry Society of America. He also serves on the Boards of Yaddo and Bennington College, the latter as Chairman. John, his wife Penny, and their three children, Nate, Chris and Jenny, live in Westchester County, New York.

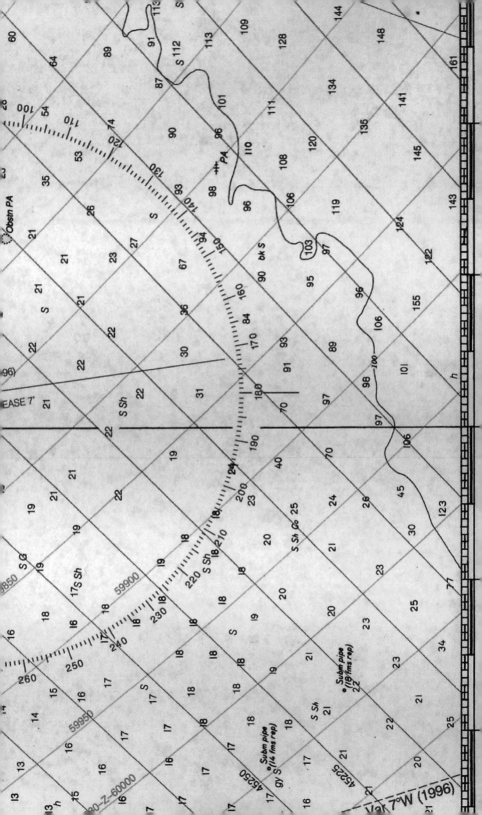